And all that jazz

Words by Fred Ebb

Improvised sounds of 1930s Chicago noisy hall – loud Ameri...
including 'Whoopee!', 'Skidoo', 'Hot', plus much laughter

© 1973 (renewed) Unichappell Music Inc and Kander & Ebb Inc, USA
Warner/Chappell North America Ltd, London W6 8BS

This music is copyright. Photocopying is ILLEGAL and is THEFT.

4

Roxie

Words by Fred Ebb

Music by John Kander
arr. Alexander L'Estrange,
based on an idea by Charles Beale

© 1974 (renewed) Unichappell Music Inc and Kander & Ebb Inc, USA
Warner/Chappell North America Ltd, London W6 8BS

This music is copyright. Photocopying is ILLEGAL and is THEFT.

When you're good to Mama

Words by Fred Ebb

Music by John Kander
arr. Alexander L'Estrange,
based on an idea by Charles Beale

Got a lit-tle mot-to,___ al-ways sees me through,

When you're good to Ma - ma,___ Ma-ma's good to you.___

There's a lot of fa - vors___ I'm pre-pared to do___

© 1975 Unichappell Music Inc and Kander & Ebb Inc, USA
Warner/Chappell North America Ltd, London W6 8BS

This music is copyright. Photocopying is ILLEGAL and is THEFT.

SOLO (opt.)

You do one for Ma - ma, She'll do one for you.

S. Aah_____ aah_____ and that's the way I

A. They say that life is 'tit for tat' and that's the way I

live. Aah_____ for what I got to give.

live. So I de-serve a lot-ta 'tat'_ for what I got to give.

Don't you know that this hand wash-es that one too.

da dat da dat dah too._____

When you're good to Ma - ma,___ Ma - ma's good to you._

doo doop pi doo   doo doop pi doo   doo doop pi doo   aah___

If you want her gra - vy,   pep - per her ra - goût._

Spice it up for Ma - ma,___ She'll get hot for you.

ah___   She'll get hot for you.

choral basics

consultant editor Alexander L'Estrange

And all that jazz: this sassy collection contains three songs from the well loved Kander and Ebb musical, *Chicago*. Enjoy the show-stopping melodies and high drama in these exciting arrangements – 'And all that jazz', 'Roxie' and 'When you're good to Mama'.

• • • • • • •

choral basics has been carefully designed to provide rewarding, varied repertoire for beginner choirs. Perfect for singers of all ages, the series offers:

- simple choral arrangements for 2 parts (soprano and alto) and 3 parts (soprano, alto and a combined male-voice part)

- an array of repertoire including world music, spirituals, pop classics, show hits and original pieces

- attractive, idiomatic arrangements, with breathing and vocal range considered for the level

- straightforward piano accompaniments, supporting the vocal lines

- great value for money, with each volume comprising a set of contrasted songs for easy programming

 So build up your confidence and kick-start your choral singing with choral basics !

Alexander L'Estrange

Also available in this series:

 **FABER ff MUSIC**

fabermusic.com

ISBN10: 0-571-52940-2
EAN13: 978-0-571-52940-7

9 780571 529407 >